EARLY INTERMEDIATE

PIANO SOLOS IN
LYRICAL STYLE

BY CAROLYN MILLER

ISBN 978-1-4803-6859-0

WILLIS MUSIC

EXCLUSIVELY DISTRIBUTED BY

HAL•LEONARD®
CORPORATION
7777 W. BLUEMOUND RD. P.O. BOX 13819 MILWAUKEE, WI 53213

Visit Hal Leonard Online at
www.halleonard.com

FROM THE COMPOSER

In my many years of teaching, I have found that students love learning dreamy, romantic solos in addition to fast, showy pieces. Lyrical melodies need to be shaped, and students want to learn to play expressively and with a beautiful tone. The sensitive side of performing needs to be developed. This collection has a variety of lyrical pieces that offer different moods and styles to stir imaginations—from falling snowflakes, to dancing island breezes, to a majestic knight's castle. The bittersweet "Remembrance" holds a special place in my heart.

It is my hope that these pieces will help develop the lyricism within each student to create beautiful, expressive and artistic performances.

Enjoy!

Carolyn Miller

Carolyn Miller's teaching and composing career spans over 40 prolific years. She holds music degrees from both the College Conservatory of Music (University of Cincinnati) and Xavier University. Carolyn's compositions appear frequently on state contest lists, as well as on the popular NFMC Festivals Bulletin. She presents workshops and showcases for Willis Music throughout the United States and adjudicates regularly at festivals and competitions. Although she recently retired from the Ohio public school system, she continues to maintain her own private studio. Carolyn is listed in the *Who's Who in America* and *Who's Who of American Women*.

CONTENTS

Dancing in the Rain

Carolyn Miller

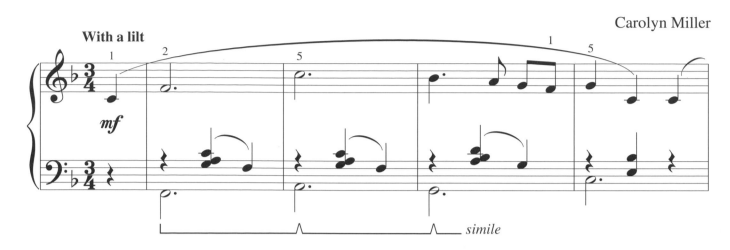

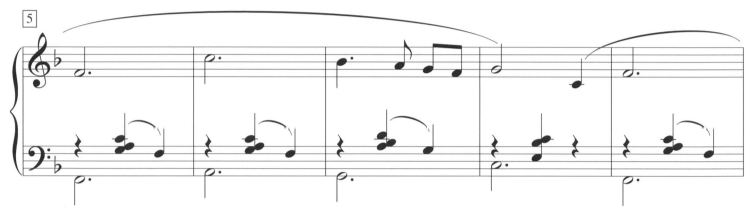

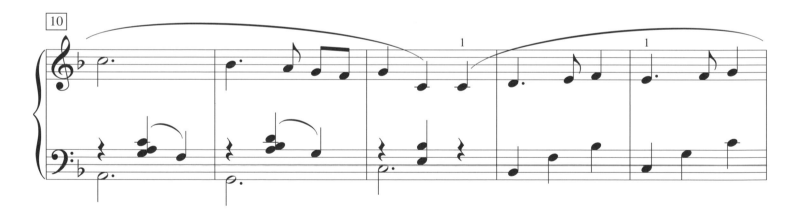

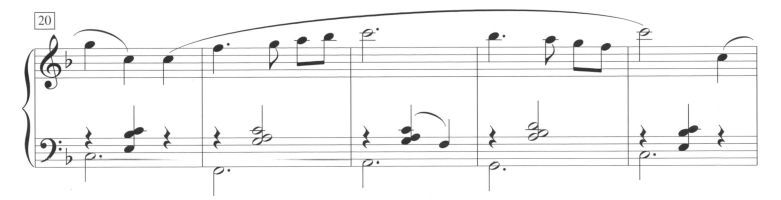

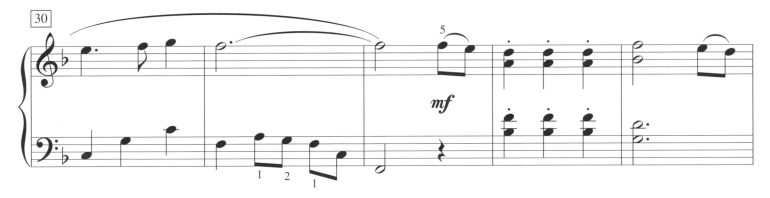

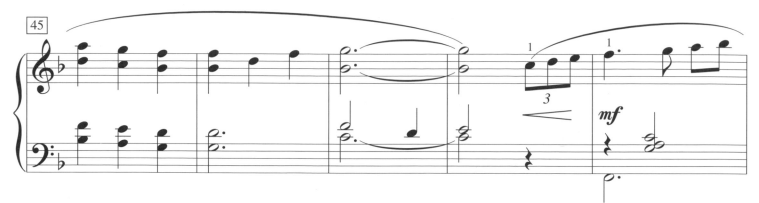

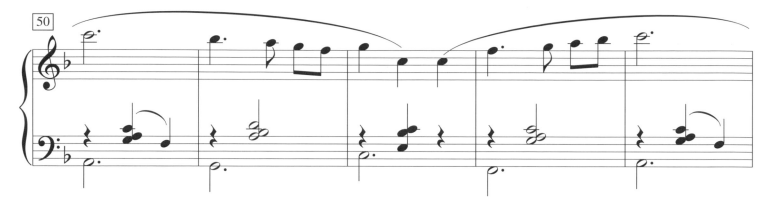

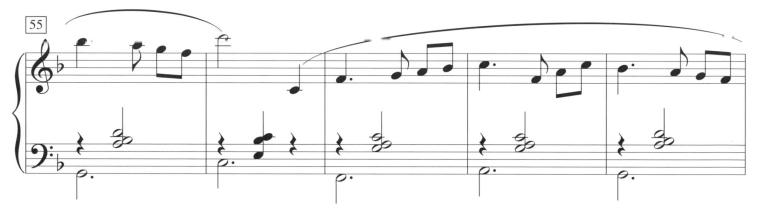

Falling Snowflakes

Carolyn Miller

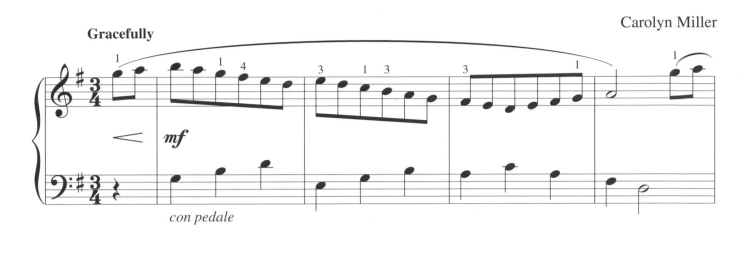

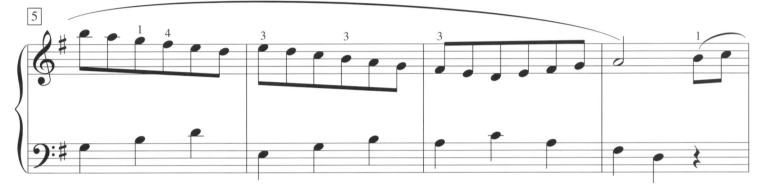

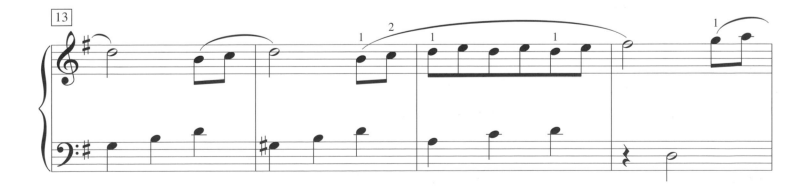

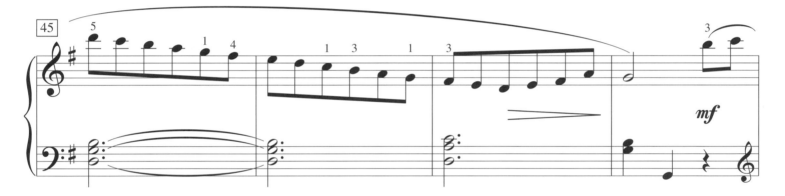

Island Breeze

Carolyn Miller

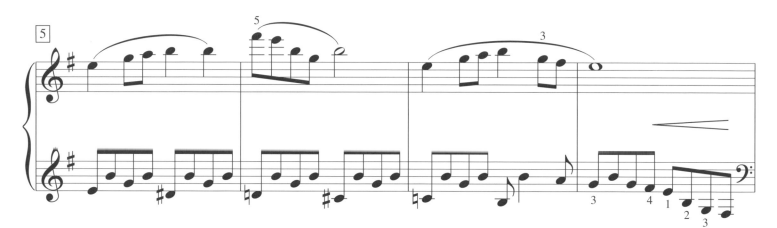

Knights of the Castle

Carolyn Miller

Majestic and brave

The knights march

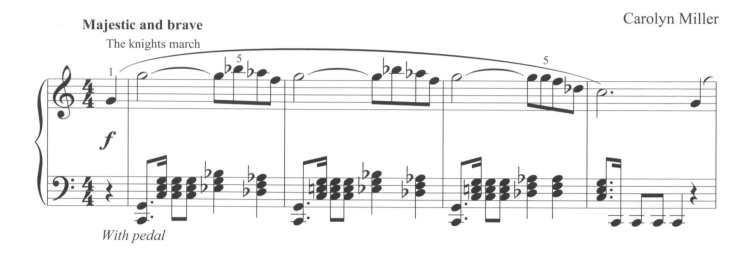

The princess appears

The knights kneel as the princess passes by

The knights resume their march

Longing

Carolyn Miller

con pedale

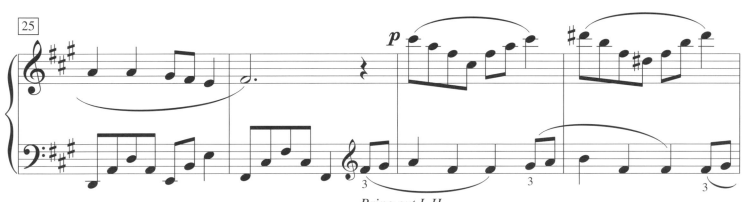

Bring out L.H.

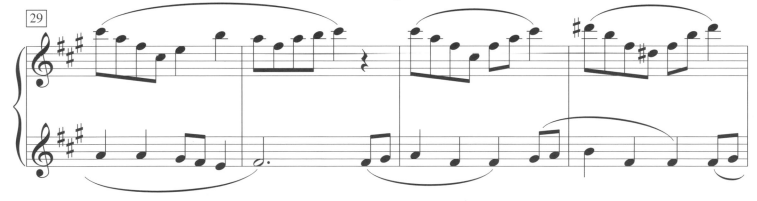

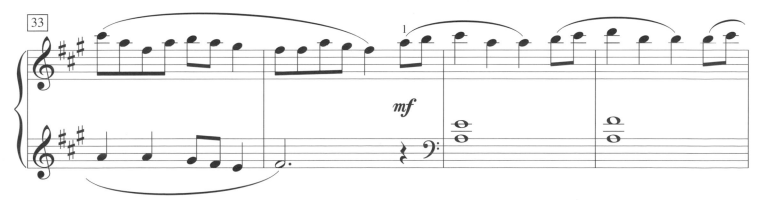

Tango Español

Carolyn Miller

Rhythmic, not too fast

mf

With light pedal

Remembrance

Carolyn Miller

Andante cantabile con rubato

con pedale

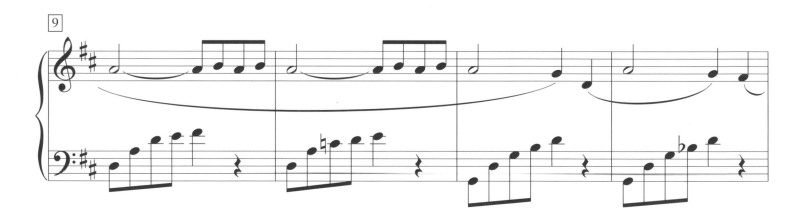

poco rit.

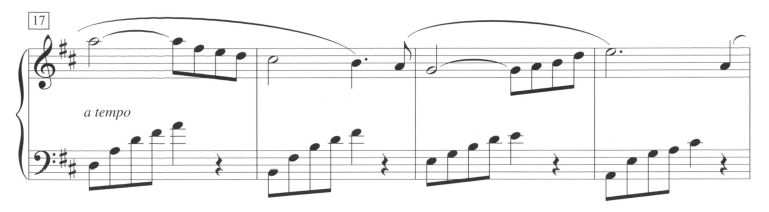

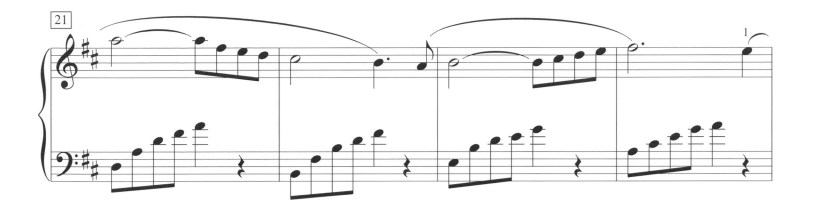

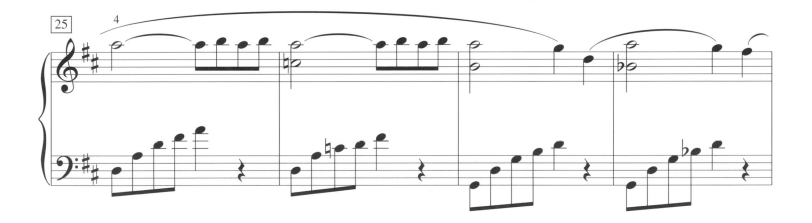

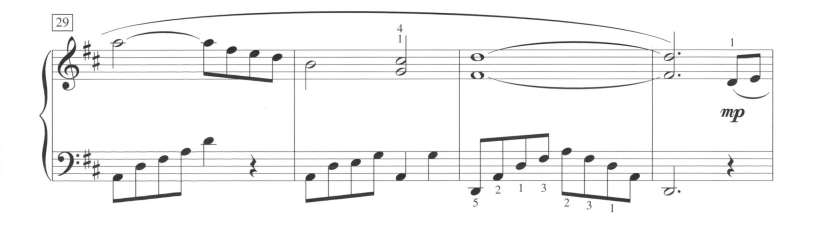

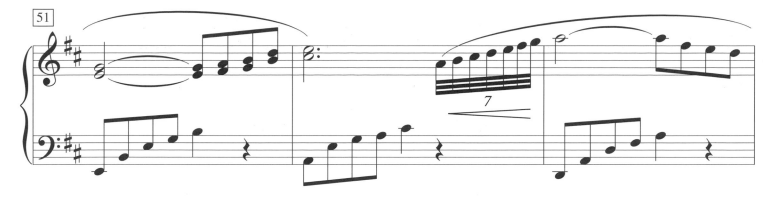

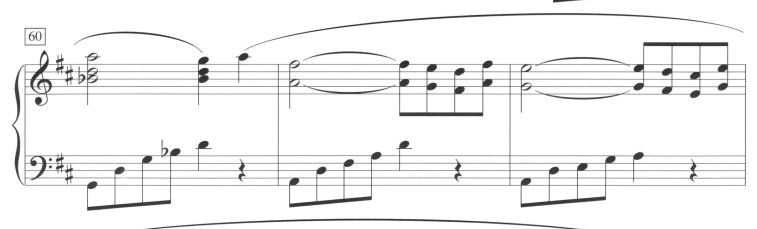

A DOZEN A DAY SONGBOOK SERIES

BROADWAY, MOVIE AND POP HITS

Arranged by Carolyn Miller

The *A Dozen a Day Songbook* series contains wonderful Broadway, movie and pop hits that may be used as companion pieces to the memorable technique exercises in the *A Dozen a Day* series. They are also suitable as supplements for ANY method!

Mini
Early Elementary

A DOZEN A DAY SONGBOOK

Broadway, Movie and Pop Hits
Any Dream Will Do • Can You Feel the Love Tonight • A Dream Is a Wish Your Heart Makes
Heigh-Ho • I'm Popeye the Sailor Man • It's a Grand Night for Singing • Lean on Me
Love Me Tender • So Long, Farewell • You'll Never Walk Alone

THE WILLIS MUSIC COMPANY

MINI
EARLY ELEMENTARY
Songs in the Mini Book:
Any Dream Will Do • Can You Feel the Love Tonight • A Dream Is a Wish Your Heart Makes • Heigh-Ho • I'm Popeye the Sailor Man • It's a Grand Night for Singing • Lean on Me • Love Me Tender • So Long, Farewell • You'll Never Walk Alone.

00416858 Book Only $7.99

00416861 Book/Audio $12.99

PREPARATORY
MID-ELEMENTARY
Songs in the Preparatory Book:
The Bare Necessities • Do-Re-Mi • Getting to Know You • Heart and Soul • Little April Shower • Part of Your World • The Surrey with the Fringe on Top • Swinging on a Star • The Way You Look Tonight • Yellow Submarine.

00416859 Book Only $7.99

00416862 Book/Audio $12.99

BOOK 1
LATER ELEMENTARY
Songs in Book 1:
Cabaret • Climb Ev'ry Mountain • Give a Little Whistle • If I Were a Rich Man • Let It Be • Rock Around the Clock • Twist and Shout • The Wonderful Thing About Tiggers • Yo Ho (A Pirate's Life for Me) • Zip-A-Dee-Doo-Dah.

00416860 Book Only $7.99

00416863 Book/Audio $12.99

BOOK 2
EARLY INTERMEDIATE
Songs in Book 2:
Hallelujah • I Dreamed A Dream • I Walk the Line • I Want to Hold Your Hand • In the Mood • Moon River • Once Upon A Dream • This Land is Your Land • A Whole New World • You Raise Me Up.

00119241 Book Only $6.99

00119242 Book/Audio $12.99

Prices, content, and availability subject to change without notice.

WILLIS MUSIC

www.willispianomusic.com   **www.facebook.com/willispianomusic**